# The Judiciary Act of 1789

*Introduction by*
*David Eisenberg, Christine R. Jordan*
*Maeva Marcus, Emily Van Tassel*

MILESTONE DOCUMENTS IN THE NATIONAL ARCHIVES

National Archives and Records Administration

Washington, DC

Published for the
National Archives and Records Administration
By the National Archives Trust Fund Board
1989


**Library of Congress Cataloging-in-Publication Data**

The Judiciary Act of 1789 / introduction by David Eisenberg et al.

    (Milestone documents in the National Archives)
       1. Courts— United States. 2. Jurisdiction— United States.
I. United States. National Archives and Records Administration.
II. Series.
KF8719.J83 1988                    88-19730
347.73′1— dc19
[347.3071]
ISBN 0-911333-74-6

# An Introduction

As the first justices of the Supreme Court were preparing to undertake their duties, President George Washington wrote to them expressing his feelings about the importance of the job they were about to begin. "I have always been persuaded that the stability and success of the National Government and consequently the happiness of the People of the United States, would depend in a considerable degree on the Interpretation and Execution of its Laws," Washington observed. "In my opinion, therefore, it is important that the Judiciary System not only be independent in its operations, but as perfect as possible in its formation."

The founders of the new nation believed that the establishment of a national judiciary was one of their most important tasks. Yet article 3 of the Constitution of the United States, the provision that deals with the judicial branch of government, is markedly shorter than articles 1 and 2, which created the legislative and executive branches. Moreover, at the Constitutional Convention the delegates spent relatively little time discussing judicial power. Instead, they left the resolution of those issues on which they could not easily agree to the new Congress. Thus the story of the development of judicial power under the Constitution concerns much more than an understanding of the text of article 3.

The concept of a national judiciary was a new one in the late 1780s, and its embodiment in article 3 was a cause of much concern. The structure of the judiciary was a rock upon which the Constitution could founder when it went before the states for ratification; hence Federalist efforts had focused on creating a constitutional framework that would give wide latitude to Congress to flesh out the particulars of a court system. By creating a structure that left all the details of form and content to congressional discretion, Federalists hoped to allay— or at least postpone until after the Constitution was safely ratified— Antifederalist fears that the national judiciary would swallow up the state courts.

Article 3 of the Constitution created a federal "judicial Power" but defined it in only the broadest of terms. Section 1 provided that power "shall be vested in one supreme Court, and in such inferior Courts as the Congress may from time to time ordain and establish." Section 2 specified the types of cases to which the federal judicial power extended, giving the Supreme Court original jurisdiction to hear "all Cases affecting Ambassadors, other public Ministers and Consuls, and those in which a State shall be a Party." In all other categories enumerated in the section, cases would originate in the lower courts but could be brought to the

Supreme Court on appeal, subject to "such exceptions, and under such Regulations as the Congress shall make." Hence the Constitution left to congressional discretion the content and extent of the appellate jurisdiction of the Supreme Court, and by implication the entire jurisdiction of any lower federal courts that might be established.

Soon after the Constitutional Convention adjourned in September 1787, people began to express fears that an extensive federal court system would prove too expensive, drag hapless defendants hundreds of miles from home, and undermine state sovereignty and individual liberties. Antifederalist forces led by

Richard Henry Lee, a member of the Continental Congress and a leading Antifederalist who refused to attend the Constitutional Convention, was appointed to the Senate committee responsible for drafting the judiciary bill.

two Virginians— George Mason, who had refused to sign the Constitution, and Richard Henry Lee, who had refused to attend the Constitutional Convention— started an immediate campaign in the press and in the state ratifying conventions to have the federal judicial power amended before ratification of the Constitution. Recalling the harsh colonial governors and British Vice-Admiralty judges in the years before the Revolution, Antifederalists were particularly concerned with protecting the rights of the criminally accused.

Even such a leading Federalist as James Madison, on the eve of his election to the House of Representatives in January 1789, acknowledged the need for some sort of bill of rights to protect individual liberties and some sort of restriction on appeals in the federal courts. As early as March 15, 1789, the staunch Massachusetts Federalist Fisher Ames reported from New York to a friend in New England that a judicial plan was being discussed by three or four persons that would limit diversity suits and suits involving foreigners to cases where the sum in controversy was over $500. He further commented that the great objectives of low cost and allaying state-federal jealousies might best be accomplished by narrowing rather than expanding federal jurisdiction.

It fell to the First Congress to interpret the various sections of article 3 and to take into consideration the amendments demanded by several states as the price of ratification. By drawing up the Bill of Rights and enacting the Judiciary Act of 1789, the First Congress met the concerns of many. It was able to establish a working judicial system that pleased no one completely, but which could be changed as experience showed it to be necessary or desirable.

While the House of Representatives began its work on the first important piece of financial legislation, a revenue system, the Senate, acknowledging the pivotal role that the federal court system must play in the new government, began its legislative work by appointing a committee to prepare a judiciary bill. The committee as formed on April 7, 1789, consisted of one senator from each state.

Only Oliver Ellsworth, William Paterson, and Caleb Strong, of the ten committee members on whom the judiciary's fate depended, could claim any sizable technical legal expertise; but most had a strong political and legislative background. Six had been members of the Continental Congress (Ellsworth, William Few, Charles Carroll of Carrollton, Ralph Izard, Paine Wingate, and Richard Henry Lee). Five had been members of the Constitutional Convention (Ellsworth, Strong, Paterson, Richard Bassett, and Few). Five had been members of their state ratifying conventions (Ellsworth, Strong, Few, Bassett, and Izard). Nearly all had held a variety of state offices. Politically all were Federalists with the exception of Richard Henry Lee, a leading Antifederalist and a harsh critic of an expansive federal judiciary, and William Maclay, who was elected by Pennsylvania to represent the state's agricultural interests.

Within three weeks the committee had drafted a set of guiding principles that clearly reflected the concerns raised during the ratification debate over limiting federal court jurisdiction. The resolutions indicated that the committee favored a small judiciary and had already adopted the idea of limiting noncriminal cases tried in federal courts to those involving large sums of money. The structure created by the committee included a Supreme Court and two levels of lower federal courts. The draft bill specified a six-judge Supreme Court, to convene twice yearly in the national capital. During the months when they were not sitting as the Supreme Court, the justices were made responsible for hearing trials and appeals on circuit in the several states, sitting in pairs in conjunction with a district court judge. The district court judges would come from the courts established in each state as federal trial courts, responsible primarily for hearing admiralty cases. The circuit court's jurisdiction in noncriminal cases was restricted in most instances to cases of at least $300 or more. Appeals to the Supreme Court could only be made in cases involving amounts above $2000. Finally, the committee gave the Supreme Court explicit powers of judicial review over state supreme court decisions involving federal law. There seemed to have been a consensus that only cases involving substantial amounts of money should be subject to federal appellate review unless an interpretation of the federal Constitution, a statute, or a treaty were in question.

The drafting efforts of Paterson, Ellsworth, and Strong culminated in a first reading before the full Senate on June 12. When printed for distribution and Senate debate, the bill ran 16 pages. District court jurisdiction, which was to give rise to the greatest debate in both houses, had been fleshed out in more detail. In addition to exclusive original jurisdiction over all civil admiralty and maritime cases, district courts were also given jurisdiction over some other lesser federal matters. The committee made trial by jury protections explicit in several situations, among them criminal cases and suits brought by the United States for amounts over $100. Similarly, jury trials were required in civil and criminal cases in the circuit courts and in original Supreme Court cases involving individuals who were United States citizens.

After agreeing to report the committee bill, Richard Henry Lee then leveled an Antifederalist attack at the jurisdiction of the district courts. On the opening day of debate, June 22, Lee moved to limit the district courts to admiralty jurisdiction. Simply stated, Lee's proposed amendment called for the judiciaries of the several states to serve as lower federal courts in most instances. While many people believed that state courts could handle the business that might be assigned to lower federal courts, opponents of this view argued that state control over the application of federal law would result in diminished popular confidence that national laws were being executed impartially. State judges who held office only for specified terms could not be relied upon to be independent, and appeals to the Supreme Court would have to be allowed in large numbers of cases to ensure the enforcement of national interests. Moreover, some argued that as soon as state judges exercised federal powers they would become federal judges, with life tenure and secure salaries as mandated by the second clause of article 3, section 1. Why Lee chose to introduce his amendment after apparently having gone along with the committee in setting up a lower court system is not known. Perhaps Lee felt obligated to bring this proposal to the attention of the full Senate because he had been so directed by the Virginia legislature. The oddity is increased by the fact that Virginia had just enacted a restriction on its courts forbidding them to try cases arising under the laws of the United States.

Even Maclay, who had been on the committee with Lee and who would join Lee in voting against the bill in its final form, did not support Lee on this point. Maclay joined with the Federalists in believing that the Constitution's scheme would be thwarted unless the federal courts could adjudicate other issues besides admiralty— such as taxation, duties and imports, naturalization, coinage, counterfeiting, and treason. He also made the longstanding Federalist point that the state judges would not enforce federal laws. William Paterson may have advanced some of the additional reasons against using state courts as federal tribunals: his personal notes reflect that he thought the elective office of most state judges was not compatible with the constitutional requirements of tenure during good behavior and fixed salaries. Paterson agreed that state judges should not be relied upon to enforce federal criminal laws or the collection of federal revenue. The Federalist majority, many of whom had already rejected the notion of state courts as lower federal courts in their correspondence with constituents, followed his view. On July 17 the Senate voted 14-6 to pass the bill.

At the same time that the Senate was considering the judiciary bill, the House had taken up the subject of a bill of rights. As originally proposed by James Madison on June 6, it included several amendments pertaining to the judicial system. Deemed most important were those protecting the rights of the criminally accused: the right to grand jury indictment; to a speedy and public trial by an impartial jury of the vicinage (i.e. vicinity in which the crime was committed); to know the cause and nature of accusations; to confront witnesses and have compulsory process to produce them; to assistance of counsel; to due process; and to protection against self-incrimination, double jeopardy, excessive bail and fines, and cruel and unusual punishment. With the exception of the jury of the vicinage, which was struck down by the Senate, all of these became parts of the fifth, sixth, and eighth amendments. Madison's list also included the three judicial system amendments considered most important by the Antifederalists: a guarantee of jury trial in common law cases (that is, suits governed by earlier judicial decisions rather than by statutes) above $20; a prohibition on the reexamination of the facts found in a case by the trial court except by the restrictive rules of the common law (which meant that jury decisions would not be easily overturned); and a monetary restriction on all appeals to the Supreme Court. The Senate removed this last provision, but the first two became the seventh amendment.

Having postponed consideration of the judiciary bill until after passage of a bill of rights, the House began debate on the former on August 27. Despite heavy speculation that Madison would lead the attack, he failed to do so and few substantial changes were made. In his closing speech on the bill, delivered on September 17, Madison summed up the views of most of his colleagues that the bill, however imperfect, was the best they could get at this late date in the session, and that it could always be changed as experience proved necessary. That day the House voted 37-16 in favor of the bill with amendments.

The only direct evidence of interaction between the two houses as they considered the judiciary bill and the bill of rights is a letter of September 24 from

Senator William Paterson of New Jersey played a significant role in preparing the first draft of the judiciary bill. The first page of the draft is in his hand.

Caleb Strong was a member of the Constitutional Convention, the Massachusetts ratifying convention, and the Senate committee charged with preparing a judiciary bill.

Madison to Edmund Pendleton discussing the bill of rights. "It will be impossible I find to prevail on the Senate to concur in limitation on the value of appeals to the Supreme Court," complained Madison,

> which they say is unnecessary, and might be embarrassing in questions of national or Constitutional importance in their principle, tho' of small pecuniary amount. They are equally inflexible in opposing a definition of the locality of Juries. The vicinage they contend is either too vague or too strict, too vague if depending on limits to be fixed by the pleasure of the law, too strict if limited to the County. . . . The Senate suppose also that the provision for vicinage in the Judiciary bill, will sufficiently quiet the fears which called for an amendment on this point.

James Madison acknowledged the need for some guidelines for the federal court system, but feared that the judiciary bill would lessen support for his proposed constitutional amendment concerning vicinage.

On September 19 the Senate disagreed to four House amendments to the judiciary bill and proposed a compromise to another to allow the trial jury in capital cases to be drawn from the county in which the crime was committed. The changes were agreed to by the House on September 21, the same day that a joint conference committee of Representatives Madison, Roger Sherman, and John Vining and Senators Ellsworth, Paterson, and Carroll was appointed to resolve the differences over the bill of rights. Three days later, on September 24, as the conference committee was agreeing to limit constitutional protection to a jury of the district, President Washington signed the Judiciary Act into law. Although little hard evidence exists to suggest that the Judiciary Act and the Bill of Rights were deliberately fashioned to complement each other, the fact is that together they took care of most Antifederalist concerns about the judiciary under the Constitution.

Probably none of the Judiciary Act's provisions captured the spirit of balancing state and federal interests better than section 34. The section stipulated, simply enough,

> [t]hat the laws of the several States except where the Constitution, treaties or statutes of the United States shall otherwise require or provide, shall be regarded as rules of decision in trials at common law in the Courts of the United States in cases where they apply.

While the First Congress may well have intended "laws of the several states" merely as a shorthand for all the laws then in effect, including the unwritten common law, it is equally possible that the framers meant "laws" to refer only to statutes, leaving the federal courts free to fashion common law remedies of their own. Even if the drafters did intend that "laws" include the common law of the several states, they may have wished merely to permit, not to compel, the federal trial courts to apply state common law. Still another possibility is that the bill's framers deliberately worded the provision vaguely so as to leave its meaning open to future judicial interpretation. Its literal meaning notwithstanding, section 34 was written, like the other sections, in the spirit of reconciling national interests with those of the various states. The enactment of the Judiciary Act of 1789 marked the culmination of an effort to implement federal law adequately and yet in a manner least detrimental to state policies and practices.

The passage of the Judiciary Act of 1789 was crucial to the growth of the federal judiciary. The remarks of Associate Justice Samuel Chase in a 1799 opinion sum up its importance. "The notion has frequently been entertained," noted Chase,

> that the federal courts derive their judicial power immediately from the Constitution; but the political truth is that the disposal of the judicial power (except in a few specified instances) belongs to Congress. If Congress has given the power to this court, we possess it, not otherwise; and if Congress has not given the power to us or to any other court, it still remains at the legislative disposal.

The generality of article 3 of the Constitution raised questions that Congress had to address in the Judiciary Act of 1789. These questions had no easy answers, and the solutions to them were achieved politically. The First Congress decided that it could regulate the jurisdiction of all federal courts, and in the Judiciary Act of 1789 Congress established with great particularity a limited jurisdiction for the district and circuit courts, gave the Supreme Court the original jurisdiction provided for in the Constitution, and granted the Court appellate jurisdiction in cases from the federal circuit courts and from state courts where those courts' rulings had rejected federal claims. The decision to grant federal courts a jurisdiction more restrictive than that allowed by the Constitution represented a recognition by the Congress that the people of the United States would not find a full-blown federal court system palatable at that time.

For nearly all of the next century the judicial system remained essentially as established by the Judiciary Act of 1789. Only after the country had expanded across a continent and had been torn apart by civil war were major changes made. A separate tier of appellate circuit courts created in 1891 removed the burden of circuit riding from the shoulders of the Supreme Court justices but otherwise left intact the judicial structure.

With minor adjustments, it is the same system we have today. Congress has continued to build on the interpretation of the drafters of the first judiciary act in exercising a discretionary power to expand or restrict federal court jurisdiction. While opinions as to what constitutes the proper balance of federal and state concerns vary no less today than they did nearly two centuries ago, the fact that today's federal court system closely resembles the one created in 1789 suggests that the First Congress performed its job admirably.

# The Facsimiles

ORIGINAL DRAFT OF THE SENATE BILL
(Record Group 46, National Archives)

These three pages are from the original handwritten draft of the bill that came out of the Senate committee. The first page is in the hand of William Paterson, the other two were penned by Oliver Ellsworth.

PRINTED SENATE BILL
Courtesy of the Library of Congress

Thomas Greenleaf printed copies of the bill for distribution among the Senators for debate.

ENGROSSED JUDICIARY ACT
(Record Group 11, National Archives)

President George Washington signed the Judiciary Act into law on September 24, 1789. The engrossed copy of the act is written on both sides of three sheets of parchment and one side of a fourth and measures approximately 26¾" by 30". Shown here are pages 1, 2, and 7.

1.

A Bill
~~...~~ establish the ~~...~~ of the
United States

Be it enacted by the Senate and
Representatives of the United States of America
in Congress assembled, That the Supreme
Court of the United States shall consist of
a Chief Justice and five ~~~~ associate Justices,
any four of whom shall be a Quorum,
and shall hold annually at the Seat of the
federal Government two Sessions, the
one commencing the first Monday in
February, and the other the first Monday
in August. That the associate Justices shall
have Precedence according to the date of
their Commissions, or where the Commissions
of two or more of them bear date on the
same Day, according to their respective ages.

2. And be it further enacted, by the authority aforesaid, that the
United States shall be and they hereby
are divided into eleven Districts to be
~~...~~ and called ~~...~~

Page 15th   X

And be it further enacted, That the ~~Statute~~ Laws
~~law~~ of the several States ~~in force for the time~~
~~being, & their ~~~~~~~~~~ and last~~~~~~~
~~~~~~~~~~~~~~~~~~~~~~~~~~~~~~~~~~
~~the of England, the ~~~~~~~~~~~~~~~~~
~~~~~~~~~~~~~~~~,~~ except where the constitution
Treaties or Statutes of the United States shall
otherwise require or provide, shall be regarded as rules of decision in ~~the~~ trials at com_
mon law in the courts of the United States
in cases where they apply.—

such clause of the said constitution, treaty, statute or commission, may be reexamined & reversed or affirmed in the Supreme court of the United States, upon a petition in error, the citation being signed by the chief Justice or Judge or chancellor of the court rendering or passing the judgment or decree complained of, or by a Justice of the supreme court of the United States, in the same manner & under the same regulations, & the petition shall have the same effect, as if the judgment or decree complained of had been rendered or passed in in a circuit court, & the proceedings upon the reversal shall also be the same, except that the Supreme Court instead of sending back the cause for a final decision as before provided, may at their discretion if the cause shall have been once so sent back before, proceed to a final decision of the same & award execution. — But no other error shall be assigned or regarded as a ground of reversal in any such case as aforesaid, than such as

# A BILL

TO ESTABLISH THE

## JUDICIAL COURTS of the UNITED STATES.

BE IT ENACTED by the senate and representatives of the United States of America in Congress assembled, That the supreme court of the United states shall consist of a chief justice and five associate justices, any four of whom shall be a quorum, and shall hold annually at the seat of the federal government two sessions, the one commencing the first Monday of February, and the other the first Monday of August. That the associate justices shall have precedence according to the date of their commissions, or when the commissions of two or more of them bear date on the same day, according to their respective ages.

AND BE IT FURTHER ENACTED by the authority aforesaid, That the United States shall be, and they hereby are divided into eleven districts to be limited and called as follows, to wit, one to consist of the state of New-Hampshire, and that part of the state of Massachusetts, which lies easterly of the state of New-Hampshire, and to be called New-Hampshire district; one to consist of the remaining part of the state of Massachusetts, and to be called Massachusetts district; one to consist of the state of Connecticut, and to be called Connecticut district; one to consist of the state of New-York, and to be called New-York district; one to consist of the state of New-Jersey, and to be called New-Jersey district; one to consist of the state of Pennsylvania, and to be called Pennsylvania district; one to consist of the state of Delaware, and to be called Delaware district; one to consist of the state of Maryland, and to be called Maryland district; one to consist of the state of Virginia, and to be called Virginia district; one to consist of the state of South-Carolina, and to be called South-Carolina district; and one to consist of the state of Georgia, and to be called Georgia district.

AND BE IT FURTHER ENACTED by the authority aforesaid, That there be a court called a district court in each of the afore-mentioned districts to consist of one judge, who shall reside in the district for which he is appointed, and shall be called a district judge, and shall hold annually four sessions, the first of which to commence as follows, to wit, in the districts of New-York, and of New-Jersey on the first, in the district of Pennsylvania on the second, in the district of Connecticut on the third,

[ 2 ]

in the districts of Delaware and of South-Carolina on the fourth Tuesdays of November next; in the districts of Massachusetts and of Maryland on the first, in the district of Georgia on the second, and in the districts of New-Hampshire and of Virginia on the third Tuesdays of December next; and the other three sessions progressively in the respective districts on the like Tuesdays of every third calendar month afterwards; and that the district judge shall have power to hold special courts at his discretion. That the stated district court shall be held at the places following, to wit, in the district of New-Hampshire alternately at Portsmouth and Portland beginning at the first; in the district of Massachusetts at Boston; in the district of Connecticut at Middle-Town; in the district of New-York at New-York; in the district of New-Jersey alternately at New-Brunswick and Burlington, beginning at the first; in the district of Pennsylvania at Philadelphia; in the district of Delaware at Dover; in the district of Maryland at Baltimore; in the district of Virginia alternately at Richmond and Williamsburgh beginning at the first; in the district of South-Carolina at Charleston; and in the district of Georgia alternately at Savannah and Augusta beginning at the first; and that the special courts shall be held at the same place in each district as the stated courts, or in districts that have two at either of them in the discretion of the judge, or at such other place in the district as the nature of the business and his discretion shall direct. And that, in the districts that have but one place for holding the district court, the records thereof shall be kept at that place, and in districts that have two, at that place in each district which the judge shall appoint.

AND BE IT FURTHER ENACTED by the authority aforesaid, That the before-mentioned district shall be divided into three circuits, and be called the eastern, the middle, and the southern circuit. That the eastern circuit shall consist of the districts of New-Hampshire, Massachusetts, Connecticut, and New-York; that the middle circuit shall consist of the districts of New-Jersey, Pennsylvania, Delaware, Maryland, and Virginia; and that the southern circuit shall consist of the districts of South-Carolina and Georgia; and that there shall be held annually in each district two courts, which shall be called circuit courts, and shall consist of any two justices of the supreme court, and the district judge of such districts any two of whom shall constitute a quorum.

AND BE IT FURTHER ENACTED by the authority aforesaid, That the first session of the said circuit court in the several districts shall commence at the times following, to wit, in New-Jersey on the second, in New-York on the fourth, in Pennsylvania on the eleventh, in

[ 3 ]

Connecticut on the twenty-second, in South-Carolina on the twenty-fifth, and in Delaware on the twenty-seventh days of April next; in Massachusetts on the third, in Maryland on the seventh, in Georgia on the tenth, in New-Hampshire on the twentieth, and in Virginia on the twenty-second days of May next, and the subsequent sessions in the respective districts on the like days of every sixth calendar month afterwards, except when any of those days shall happen on a Sunday, and then the session shall commence on the next day following. And the sessions of the said circuit court shall be held in the district of New-Hampshire alternately at Portsmouth and Portland beginning at the first; in the district of Massachusetts at Boston; in the district of Connecticut at Middle-Town; in the district of New-York alternately at New-York and Albany beginning at the first; in the district of New-Jersey at Trenton; in the district of Pennsylvania at Philadelphia; in the district of Delaware alternately at New-Castle and Dover beginning at the first; in the district of Maryland alternately at Annapolis and Easton beginning at the first; in the district of Virginia alternately at Richmond and Williamsburgh beginning at the first; in the district of South-Carolina alternately at Charleston and Cambden beginning at the first; and in the district of Georgia at Augusta.

AND BE IT FURTHER ENACTED by the authority aforesaid, That the supreme court may, by any one or more of its justices being present, be adjourned from day to day until a quorum be convened; and that a circuit court may also be adjourned from day to day by any one of its judges until a quorum be convened; and that a district court, in case of the inability of the judge to attend at the commencement of a session, may, by virtue of a written order from the said judge directed to the marshal of the district, be adjourned by the said marshal to such day, antecedent to the next stated session of the said court, as in the said order shall be appointed; and in case of the death of the said judge, and his vacancy not being supplied, all process, pleadings, and proceedings of what nature soever pending before the said court shall be continued of course until the next stated session.

AND BE IT ENACTED by the authority aforesaid, That the supreme court and the district courts shall have power to appoint clerks for their respective courts; and that the clerk of each district court shall be clerk also of the circuit court in such district; and each of the said clerks shall, before he enters upon the excution of his office, take the following oath or affirmation, to wit.

" I A. B. being appointed clerk of       do solemn-
" ly swear or affirm, that I will truly and faithfully enter

" and record all the orders, decrees, judgments, and pro-
" ceedings of the said court, and that I will faithfully and
" impartially discharge and perform all the duties of my
" said office, according to the best of my abilities, and un-
" derstanding. So help me God."

AND BE IT FURTHER ENACTED by the authority aforesaid, That the justices of the supreme court and the district judges, before they proceed to execute the duties of their respective offices, shall take the following oath or affirmation, to wit.

" I A. B. do solemnly swear or affirm, that I will admi-
" nister justice without respect to persons, and do equal
" right to the poor and to the rich, and that I will faith-
" fully and impartially discharge and perform all the du-
" ties incumbent on me as
" according to the best of my abilities and understanding,
" agreeably to the constitution and laws of the United
" States. So help me God."

AND BE IT FURTHER ENACTED, That in all cases wherein by law an oath shall be allowed, authorized, directed, or required, the solemn affirmation of any of the people called Quakers shall be allowed and taken instead of such oath.

AND BE IT FURTHER ENACTED, That the district courts shall have, exclusively of the courts of the several states, cognizance of all crimes and offences that shall be cognizable under the authority of the United States, and defined by the laws of the same, committed within their respective districts, or upon the high seas; where other corporal punishment than whipping, not exceeding (30) stripes, a higher fine than (100) dollars, or a longer term of imprisonment than (6) months, is not to be inflicted; except where the laws of the United States shall otherwise direct; and the trial of facts shall be by jury.—And shall also have exclusive original cognizance of all civil causes of admiralty and maritime jurisdiction, including all seizures under laws of impost, navigation, or trade of the United States, where the seizures are made, on waters which are navigable from the sea by vessels of ten or more tons burthen, within their respective districts as well as upon the high seas.—Saving to suitors, in all cases, the right of a common law remedy where the common law is competent to give it.—And shall also have cognizance, concurrent with the courts of the several states, or the circuit courts, as the case may be, of all causes where a foreigner sues for a tort only in violation of the law of nations or a treaty of the United States.—And shall also have cognizance, concurrent as last mentioned, of all suits at common law where the United States, or a common informer as well for himself as the United States, sue, and the matter in dispute amounts, exclusive of costs, to the sum or value of (100) dollars. And the trial of facts in both cases last mentioned shall be by jury.

AND BE IT FURTHER ENACTED, That the circuit courts shall have original cognizance, concurrent with the courts of the several states, or the supreme court, as the case may be, of all suits of a civil nature at common law or in equity, where the matter in dispute exceeds, exclusive of costs, the sum or value of (500) dollars and the United States are plaintiffs or petitioners ; or a foreigner or citizen of another state than that in which the suit is brought, is a party.—And shall have exclusively cognizance of all crimes and offences cognizable under the authority of the United States, and defined by the laws of the same, except where this act otherwise provides, or the laws of the United States shall otherwise direct, and concurrent jurisdiction with the district courts of the crimes and offences cognizable therein.—But no person shall be arrested in one district for trial in another, in any civil action before a circuit or district court. And no civil suit shall be brought before either of said courts against an inhabitant of the United States by any original process in any other district than that whereof he is an inhabitant, or in which he shall be found at the time of serving the writ ; nor shall any district or circuit court have cognizance of any action to recover the contents of any promissory note or other chose in action in favor of an assignee, unless an action might have been prosecuted in such court to recover the said contents if no assignment had been made. And the circuit courts shall also have appellate jurisdiction from the district courts under the regulations and restrictions herein after provided.

AND BE IT FURTHER ENACTED, That if a suit be commenced in any state court against a foreigner, or citizen of another state than that in which the suit is brought, and the matter in dispute exceeds the aforesaid sum, or value of (500) dollars, exclusive of costs ; and such foreigner or citizen shall, at the time of entering his appearance in such state court, file a motion for the removal of the cause for trial into the next circuit court to be held in the district where the suit is pending, and offer good and sufficient surety for his entering in such circuit court, on the first day of its session, copies of said process against him, and also for his there appearing in the cause if special bail was originally requisite therein ; it shall then be the duty of the state court to accept the surety, and dismiss further proceedings in the cause ; and any bail that may have been originally taken shall be discharged ; and the said copies being entered as aforesaid in the circuit court, the cause shall there proceed in the same manner

[ 6 ]

as if it had been brought there by original process. And any attachment of the goods or estate of the defendant by the original process, shall still hold to respond the final judgment. And if in any action commenced in a state court the title of land be concerned, and the parties are citizens of the same state, and the matter in dispute exceeds the sum or value of (500) dollars, exclusive of costs, the sum or value being made to appear to the satisfaction of the court, and the defendant in his plea in bar shall set up a title under a grant from another state than that in which the suit is pending, and move that the plaintiff also set forth his title, the plaintiff shall set it forth in his replication, and if he founds it upon a grant from the state in which the suit is pending; the defendant may then, on motion, have the cause removed to the circuit court for trial, in the same manner and under the same regulations as in the case before mentioned of the removal of a cause into that court by a foreigner. And the defendant shall in such case abide by his plea in bar. And the trial of facts in the circuit courts shall, in all suits, except those of equity and of admiralty and maritime jurisdiction, be by jury.

AND BE IT FURTHER ENACTED by the authority aforesaid, That the supreme court shall have exclusive jurisdiction of all controversies of a civil nature, where any of the United States or a foreign state is a party, except between a state and its citizens; and except also between a state and citizens of other states or foreigners, in which latter case it shall have original but not exclusive jurisdiction. And shall have exclusively all such jurisdiction of suits or proceedings against ambassadors, other public ministers or consuls, or their domestics or domestic servants, as a court of law can have or exercise consistently with the law of nations; and original, but not exclusive jurisdiction of all suits for trespasses brought by ambassadors, other public ministers or consuls, or their domestics or domestic servants. And the trial of facts in the supreme court, in all actions at law against citizens of the United States, shall be by jury. The supreme court shall also have appellate jurisdiction from the circuit courts and courts of the several states, in the cases herein after specially provided for. And shall have power to issue writs of prohibition to the district courts when proceeding as courts of admiralty and maritime jurisdiction; and writs of MANDAMUS, in cases warranted by the principles and usages of law, to any courts appointed, or persons holding office, under the authority of the United States.

AND BE IT FURTHER ENACTED, That all the before mentioned courts of the United States shall have

[ 7 ]

power to issue writs of SCIRE FACIAS, HABEAS CORPUS, and all other writs not specially provided for by statute, which may be necessary for the exercise of their respective jurisdictions, and agreeable to the principles and usages of law. And that either of the justices of the supreme court, as well as judges of the district courts, shall have power to grant writs of HABEAS CORPUS for the purpose of an enquiry into the cause of commitment.—Provided that writs of HABEAS CORPUS shall in no case extend to prisoners in gaol, unless where they are in custody under or by colour of the authority of the United States, or are committed for trial before some court of the same, or are necessary to be brought into court to testify.

AND BE IT FURTHER ENACTED by the authority aforesaid, that all the said courts of the United States, shall have power in the trial of actions at law, on motion and due notice thereof being given, to require the parties to produce books or papers in their possession or power which contain evidence pertinent to the issue, in cases and under circumstances where they might be compelled to produce the same by the ordinary rules of proceeding in chancery; or, on motion of a plaintiff, and due notice thereof as aforesaid, and his rendering it probable to the satisfaction of the court that he has by casualty, and without fault or negligence of his own been deprived of evidence necessary to support his action, to require the defendant to disclose on oath his or her knowledge in the cause, in cases and under circumstances where a respondent might be compelled to make such disclosure on oath by the aforesaid rules of proceeding in chancery: And if a plaintiff shall fail to comply with such order, to produce books or papers, it shall be lawful for the courts respectively, on motion, to give the like judgment for the defendant as in cases of nonsuit; and if a defendant shall fail to comply with such order, either to produce books or papers, or to disclose on oath, it shall be lawful for the courts respectively, on motion as aforesaid to give judgment against him or her by default.

AND BE IT FURTHER ENACTED by the authority aforesaid, That suits in equity shall not be sustained in either of the courts of the United States, in any case where remedy may be had at law.

AND BE IT FURTHER ENACTED, That all the said courts of the United States shall have power to grant new trials, in cases where there has been a trial by jury, for reasons for which new trials have usually been granted in the courts of law: And shall have power to impose and administer all necessary oaths, and to punish by fine or imprisonment, at the discretion of said courts, all contempts of authority in any cause or hearing before the

[ 8 ]

same; and to make and establish all necessary rules for the orderly conducting business in the said courts, provided such rules are not repugnant to the laws of the United States.

AND BE IT FURTHER ENACTED by the authority aforesaid, that when in a circuit court, judgment upon a verdict in a civil action shall be entered, execution may, on motion of either party, at the discretion of the court, and on such conditions for the security of the adverse party as they may judge proper, be stayed (42)        days from the time of entering judgment, to give time to file in the clerk's office of said court, a motion for a new trial. And if such motion be there filed within said term of (42)        days, with a certificate thereon from either of the judges of such court, that he allows the same to be filed, which certificate he may make or refuse at his discretion, execution shall of course be further stayed to the next session of said court. And if a new trial be granted the former judgment shall be thereby rendered void.

AND BE IT FURTHER ENACTED, That where in a circuit court, a plaintiff in an action, originally brought there, or a petitioner in equity, other than the United States, recovers less than the sum or value of (500) dollars, or a libellant, upon his own appeal less than the sum or value of (300)        dollars, he shall not be allowed, but shall pay costs.

AND BE IT FURTHER ENACTED by the authority aforesaid, That from final decrees in a district court in causes of admiralty and maritime jurisdiction where the matter in dispute exceeds the sum or value of (300)        dollars, exclusive of costs, an appeal shall be allowed to the next circuit court to be held in such district.

AND BE IT FURTHER ENACTED, That final degrees and judgments in civil actions in a district court where the matter in dispute exceeds the sum or value of (50) dollars, exclusive of costs, may be re-examined, and reversed or affirmed in a circuit court holden in the same district, upon a petition in error, containing an authenticated transcript of the record, an assignment of errors, and prayer for reversal, with a citation to the adverse party annexed signed by the judge of such district court or a justice of the supreme court, the adverse party having at least (20)        days notice. And upon a like process, may final judgments and decrees in civil actions and suits in equity in a circuit court brought there by original process or removed there from courts of the several states, or if the matter in dispute exceeds the sum or value of (2000) dollars exclusive of costs, removed there by appeal from a district court; be re-examined and reversed or affirmed in the supreme court, the citation being in such case signed by

[ 9 ]

a judge of such circuit court or justice of the supreme court, and the adverse party having at least (30) days notice.—But there shall be no reversal in either court for error in ruling any plea in abatement, other than to the jurisdiction of the court, or such plea to a petition or bill in equity as is in nature of a demurrer. And petitions in error shall not be brought but within (3) years after rendering or passing the judgment or decree complained of, or in case the person entitled to such petition in error be NON COMPOS MENTIS or imprisoned, then within three years as aforesaid, exclusive of the time of such insanity or imprisonment.—And every justice or judge signing a citation on any petition in error as aforesaid shall take good and sufficient security, that the petitioner shall prosecute his petition to effect, and answer all damages and costs if he fail to make his plea good.

AND BE IT FURTHER ENACTED, That petitions in error as aforesaid shall be a SUPERSEDEAS and stay execution in cases only where the matter in dispute, exclusive of costs, exceeds, if in a district court, the sum or value of (300) dollars, or if in a circuit court, the sum or value of (2000) dollars, and the petition is served, by a copy thereof being lodged for the adverse party, in the clerk's office where the record remains, within (10) days, Sundays exclusive, after rendering the judgment or passing the decree complained of.—Until the expiration of which term of (10) days, executions shall not issue in any case where a petition in error may be a SUPERSEDEAS.—And where the matters in dispute do not, in the respective courts, exceed the several sums aforesaid, petitioners in error, failing of a reversal, shall pay double costs. And where upon a petition in error that has stayed execution the supreme or a circuit court shall affirm a judgment or decree, they shall adjudge or decree to the respondent in error just damages for his delay, as well as his costs.

AND BE IT FURTHER ENACTED by the authority aforesaid, That when a judgment or decree shall be reversed in a circuit court, such court shall proceed to render such judgment or pass such decree as the district court should have rendered or passed; and the supreme court shall do the same on reversals therein, except where the reversal is in favour of the plaintiff or petitioner in the original suit, and the damages to be assessed, or matter to be decreed, are uncertain, in which case they shall send the cause back for a final decision. And the supreme court shall not issue execution in causes that are removed before them by petitions in error, but shall send a special mandate to the circuit court to award execution thereupon.

AND BE IT FURTHER ENACTED by the authority aforesaid, That a final judgment or decree in any suit, in the

C

highest court of law or equity of a state in which a decision in the suit could be had ; where is drawn in question the validity of a treaty or statute of, or an authority exercised under the United States, and the decision is against their validity ; or where is drawn in question the validity of a statute of, or an authority exercised under any state, on the ground of their being repugnant to the constitution, treaties or laws of the United States, and the decision is in favour of such their validity ; or where is drawn in question the construction of any clause of the constitution, or of a treaty or statute of, or commission held under the United States, and the decision is against the title, right, privilege or exemption specially set up or claimed by either party, under such clause of the said constitution, treaty, statute or commission; may be re-examined and reversed or affirmed in the supreme court of the United States, upon a petition in error, the citation being signed by the chief justice or judge or chancellor of the court rendering or passing the judgment or decree complained of, or by a justice of the supreme court of the United States, in the same manner and under the same regulations, and the petition shall have the same effect, as if the judgment or decree complained of had been rendered or passed in a circuit court ; and the proceedings upon the reversal shall also be the same, except that the supreme court instead of sending back the cause for a final decision as before provided, may at their discretion, if the cause shall have been once so sent back before, proceed to a final decision of the same, and award execution. But no other error shall be assigned or regarded as a ground of reversal in any such case as aforesaid, than such as immediately respect the before-mentioned questions of validity or construction of the said constitution, treaties, statutes, commissions or authorities in dispute.

AND BE IT FURTHER ENACTED, That in all causes brought before either of the courts of the United States to recover the forfeiture annexed to any articles of agreement, covenant, bond or other specialty, where the forfeiture breach or non-performance shall be found by jury, by the default or confession of the defendant, or upon demurrer, the court before whom the action is, shall render judgment therein for the plaintiff to recover so much as is due according to equity.

AND BE IT FURTHER ENACTED, That a marshall shall be appointed in and for each district, for the term of four years; but shall be removeable from office at pleasure; whose duty it shall be, to attend the district and circuit courts when sitting therein, and also the supreme court in the district in which that court shall sit : And to execute thoughout the district, all lawful precepts directed to him, and issued under the authority of the United States; and he shall have power to command all necessary assistance in the execution of his duty, and to appoint, as there shall be occasion, one or more deputies, who shall be removeable from office by the judge of the district court, or the circuit court sitting within the district at the pleasure of either; and before he enters on the duties of his office, he shall become bound for the faithful performance of the same, by himself and by his deputies, before the judge of the district court, to the treasurer of the United States, jointly and severally, with two good and sufficient sureties, inhabitants and freeholders of such district, to be approved by the district judge, in the sum of (30,000) dollars, and shall take before said judge as shall also his deputies, before they enter on the duties of their appointment, the following oath of office:

I, A. B. do solemnly swear or affirm, that I will faithfully execute all lawful precepts directed to the marshall of the district of             under the authority of the United States, and true returns make, and in all things well and truly, and without malice or partiality, perform the duties of the office of marshall (or marshall's deputy as the case may be) of the district of             during my continuance in said office, and take only my lawful fees. So help me God.

And in all causes wherein the marshall or his deputy shall be a party, the writs and precepts therein, shall be directed to such disinterested person, as the court or any justice thereof may appoint: And the person so appointed is hereby authorised to execute and return the same: And in case of the death of any marshall, his deputy or deputies shall continue in office, unless otherwise specially removed; and shall execute the same, in the name of the deceased, until another marshall be appointed and sworn: And the defaults or misfeasances in office of such deputy or deputies in the mean time as well as before, shall be adjudged a breach of the condition of the bond given as before directed by the marshall who appointed them; and the executor or administrator of the deceased marshall shall have like remedy for the defaults and misfeasances in office of such deputy or deputies during such interval, as they would be entitled to if the marshall had continued in life and in the exercise of his said office, until his successor was appointed and sworn: And every marshall or his deputy, when removed from office, or when the term for which the marshall is appointed shall expire, shall have power notwithstanding to execute all such precepts as may be in their hands respectively at the time of such removal or expiration of office, and the marshall shall be held answerable for the delivery to his successor of all prisoners

[ 12 ]

which may be in his cuſtody at the time of his removal, or when the term for which he is appointed ſhall expire, and for that purpoſe may retain ſuch priſoners in his cuſtody until his ſucceſſor ſhall be appointed and qualified as the law directs.

AND BE IT FURTHER ENACTED, That grand and petit jurors who ſhall be ſummoned to ſerve in the courts of the United States, ſhall have the ſame qualifications as are requiſite for jurors by the laws of the ſtate of which they are citizens, to ſerve in the higheſt courts of law of ſuch ſtate, and ſhall be returned as there ſhall be occaſion for them, from ſuch parts of the diſtrict from time to time as ſhall be moſt favorable to an impartial trial, and as the court ſhall direct, ſo as not to incur an unneceſſary expenſe or unduly to burthen the citizens of any part of the diſtrict with ſuch ſervices. And writs of VENIRE FACIAS when directed by the court ſhall iſſue from the clerk's office and ſhall be ſerved and returned by the marſhall in his proper perſon or by his deputy out of ſuch liſt as ſhall be given him by the marſhall, or in caſe the marſhall or his deputy is not an indifferent perſon or is intereſted in the event of the cauſe, by ſuch fit perſon as the court ſhall ſpecially appoint for that purpoſe, to whom they ſhall adminiſter an oath that he will truly and impartially ſerve and return ſuch writ. And when from challenges or otherwiſe there ſhall not be a jury to determine any civil or criminal cauſe, the marſhall or his deputy ſhall, by order of the court where ſuch defect of jurors ſhall happen, return jurymen DE TALIBUS CIRCUMSTANTIBUS ſufficient to complete the pannel; and when the marſhall or his deputy are diſqualified as aforeſaid, jurors may be returned by ſuch diſintereſted perſon as the court ſhall appoint.

AND BE IT FURTHER ENACTED by the authority aforeſaid, That the mode of proof by oral teſtimony and examination of witneſſes in open court ſhall be the ſame in all the courts of the United States, as well in the trial of cauſes in equity and of admiralty and maritime juriſdiction as of actions at common law. And when the teſtimony of any perſon ſhall be neceſſary in any civil cauſe depending in any diſtrict in any court of the United States, who ſhall live out of ſuch diſtrict, and at a greater diſtance from the place of trial than one hundred miles, or is bound on a voyage to ſea, or is about to go out of the United States or out of ſuch diſtrict, and to a greater diſtance from the place of trial than as aforeſaid, before the time of trial, the depoſition of ſuch perſon may be taken DE BENE ESSE before any juſtice or judge of any of the courts of the United States, or before any chancellor, juſtice or judge of a ſupreme or ſuperior court, mayor of a city, or judge of a county court or court of common pleas of any of the United States not being of counsel or attorney to either of the parties, or interested in the event of the cause; provided that a notification from the magistrate before whom the deposition is to be taken to the adverse party, to be present at the taking of the same, and to put interrogatories if he think fit, be first made out and served on the adverse party or his attorney as either may be nearest, if either is within such district, or within one hundred miles of the place of such caption, allowing time for their attendance after notified, not less than at the rate of one day, Sundays exclusive, for every twenty miles travel. And in causes of admiralty and maritime jurisdiction, when a libel shall be filed, in which an adverse party is not named, and depositions of persons circumstanced as aforesaid shall be taken before a claim be put in, the like notification as aforesaid shall be given to the person having the agency or possession of the property libelled at the time of the capture or seizure of the same, if known to the libellant. And every person deposing as aforesaid shall be carefully examined and cautioned, and sworn to testify the whole truth, and shall subscribe the testimony by him or her given after the same shall be reduced to writing, which shall be done only by the magistrate taking the deposition, or by the deponent in his presence. And the depositions so taken shall be retained by such magistrate, until he deliver the same with his own hand into the court for which they are taken; or shall, together with a certificate of the reasons as aforesaid of their being taken, and of the notice if any given to the adverse party, be by him the said magistrate sealed up and directed to such court, and remain under his seal until opened in court. And any person may be compelled to depose as aforesaid in the same manner as to appear and testify in court. And in the trial of any cause of admiralty or maritime jurisdiction in a district court, the decree in which may be appealed from, if either party shall suggest to and satisfy the court that probably it will not be in his power to produce the witnesses there testifying, before the circuit court should an appeal be had, and shall move that their testimony be taken down in writing, it shall be so done by the clerk of the court: And if an appeal be had, such testimony may be used on the trial of the same, if it shall appear to the satisfaction of the court which shall try the appeal, that the witnesses are then gone out of the United States, or out of the district where the trial is, and to a greater distance than as aforesaid from the place where the court is sitting, or that by reason of age, sickness, bodily infirmity or imprisonment they are unable to travel and appear at court, but not otherwise: And unless the same shall be made to appear on the trial of any cause,

D

with respect to witnesses whose depositions may have been taken therein, such depositions shall not be admitted or used in the cause. Provided that nothing herein shall be construed to prevent any court of the United States from granting a DEDIMUS POTESTATEM, to take depositions according to common usage, when it may be necessary to prevent a failure or delay of justice; which power they shall severally possess; nor to extend to depositions taken in PERPETUAM REI MEMORIAM, which, if they relate to matters that may be cognizable in any court of the United States, a circuit court, on application thereto made as a court of equity, may, according to the usages in chancery, direct to be taken.

AND BE IT ENACTED, That where any suit shall be depending in any court of the United States, and either of the parties shall die before final judgement, the executor or administrator of such deceased party who was plaintiff, petitioner, or defendant, in case the cause of action doth by law survive, shall have full power to prosecute or defend any such suit or action until final judgment; and the defendant or defendants are hereby obliged to answer thereto accordingly; and the court before whom such cause may be depending is hereby impowered and directed to hear and determine the same, and to render judgment for or against the estate of the deceased in the hands of such executor or administrator, as the case may require. And if such executor or administrator having been duly served with a SCIRE FACIAS from the office of the clerk of the court where such suit is depending (20) days before hand, shall neglect or refuse to become a party to the suit, the court may render judgment against the estate of the deceased party, in the same manner as if the executor or administrator had voluntarily made himself a party to the suit: And the executor or administrator who shall become a party as aforesaid, shall, upon motion to the court where the suit is depending, be entitled to a continuance of the same until the next term of the said court. And if there be two or more plaintiffs or defendants, and one or more of them shall die, if the cause of action shall survive to the surviving plaintiff or plaintiffs, or against the surviving defendant or defendants, the writ or action shall not be thereby abated; but such death being suggested upon the record, the action shall proceed at the suit of the surviving plaintiff or plaintiffs against the surviving defendant or defendants.

AND BE IT FURTHER ENACTED, That no summons, writ, declaration, return, process, judgment, or other proceedings in any of the courts of the United States, shall be abated, arrested, quashed or reversed, for any defect or want of form, but the said courts respectively shall proceed and give judgment according as the right of the cause and matter in law shall appear unto them, without regarding any imperfections, defects, or want of form in such writ, declaration or other pleading, return, process, judgment, or course of proceeding whatsoever, except those only in cases of demurrer, which the party demurring shall specially set down and express together with his demurrer as the cause thereof: And the said courts respectively shall and may, by virtue of this act from time to time, amend all and every such imperfections, defects and wants of form, other than those only which the party demurring shall express as aforesaid.

AND BE IT FURTHER ENACTED by the authority aforesaid, That every justice of the supreme court, and judge of a district court, may either upon his own knowledge, or the complaint of others, cause any person to be apprehended for any offence against the laws of the United States, and brought before himself for examination; and if he shall think proper, may bail or commit such offender or send him by warrant to the district where the offence was committed. And for any crime or offence against the laws of the United States, the offender may, by any justice of the peace, or other magistrate of any of the United States where he may be found, agreeably to the mode of process against offenders in such state accustomed, and at the expence of the United States, be arrested and imprisoned or bailed as the case may be, for trial before such court of the United States as by this act has cognizance of the offence: And copies of the process shall be returned as speedily as may be into the clerk's office of such court, together with the recognizances of the witnesses for their appearance to testify in the case; which recognizances the magistrate before whom the examination shall be, may require on pain of imprisonment: And if such commitment of the offender, or the witnesses shall be in a district other than that in which the offence is to be tried, it shall be the duty of the judge of that district where the delinquent is imprisoned, seasonably to issue, and of the marshall of the same district to execute a warrant for the removal of the offender and the witnesses, or either of them, as the case may be, to the district in which the trial is to be had. And upon all arrests in criminal cases, bail shall be admitted, except where the punishment may be death, in which cases it shall not be admitted but by the supreme or a circuit court, or two justices of the supreme court, or one justice of the supreme and a judge of a district court, who shall exercise their discretion therein, regarding the nature and circumstances of the offence, and of the evidence, and the usages of law.

[ 16 ]

AND BE IT FURTHER ENACTED, That in all the courts of the United States, the parties may plead and manage their own causes personally or by the assistance of such counsel or attornies at law as by the rules of the said courts respectively shall be permitted to manage and conduct causes therein. And each district court shall appoint a meet person, learned in the law, to act as attorney for the United States in such district, and shall swear him to the faithful execution of his office, whose duty it shall be to prosecute in such district all delinquents for crimes and offences, cognizable under the authority of the United States, and all civil actions in which the United States shall be concerned, except before the supreme court in the district in which that court shall be holden: And he shall receive as a compensation for his services such fees as shall be taxed therefor in the respective courts before which the suits or prosecutions shall be. And the supreme court shall also appoint a meet person, learned in the law, to act as attorney general for the United States, and shall swear him to a faithful execution of his office; whose duty it shall be to prosecute and conduct all suits in such court in which the United States shall be concerned, and to give his advice and opinion upon questions of law when required by the president of the United States, or when requested by the heads of any of the departments, touching any matters that may concern their departments; and shall receive such compensation for his services as shall by law be provided.

[NEW-YORK, PRINTED BY THOMAS GREENLEAF.]

## Congress of the United States

begun and held at the City of New York on
Wednesday the fourth of March one thousand seven hundred and eighty nine.

### An Act to establish the Judicial Courts of the United States.

*Be it enacted by the Senate and House of Representatives of the United States of America in Congress assembled,* That the Supreme Court of the United States shall consist of a Chief Justice and five Associate Justices, any four of whom shall be a quorum, and shall hold annually at the seat of government two sessions, the one commencing the first Monday of February, and the other the first Monday of August. That the associate Justices shall have precedence according to the date of their commissions, or when the commissions of two or more of them bear date on the same day, according to their respective ages.

*And be it further enacted,* That the United States shall be, and they hereby are divided into thirteen districts, to be limited and called as follows, to wit: one to consist of that part of the State of Massachusetts which lies easterly of the State of New Hampshire, and to be called Maine district, one to consist of the State of New Hampshire, and to be called New Hampshire district, one to consist of the remaining part of the State of Massachusetts, and to be called Massachusetts district, one to consist of the State of Connecticut, and to be called Connecticut district, one to consist of the State of New York, and to be called New York district, one to consist of the State of New Jersey, and to be called New Jersey district, one to consist of the State of Pennsylvania, and to be called Pennsylvania district, one to consist of the State of Delaware, and to be called Delaware district, one to consist of the State of Maryland, and to be called Maryland district, one to consist of the State of Virginia, except that part called the District of Kentucky, and to be called Virginia district, one to consist of the remaining part of the State of Virginia, and to be called Kentucky district, one to consist of the State of South Carolina, and to be called South Carolina district, and one to consist of the State of Georgia, and to be called Georgia district.

*And be it further enacted,* That there be a Court called a District Court in each of the afore mentioned districts, to consist of one judge, who shall reside in the district for which he is appointed, and shall be called a district judge, and shall hold annually four sessions, the first of which to commence as follows, to wit: in the districts of New York and of New Jersey on the first, in the district of Pennsylvania on the second, in the district of Connecticut on the third, and in the district of Delaware on the fourth Tuesdays of November next, in the districts of Massachusetts, of Maine and of Maryland on the first, in the district of Georgia on the second, and in the districts of New Hampshire, of Virginia and of Kentucky on the third Tuesdays of December next, and the other three sessions progressively in the respective districts on the like Tuesdays of every third calendar month afterwards, and in the district of South Carolina, on the third Monday in March and September, the first Monday in July, and the second Monday in December of each and every year, commencing in December next, and that the district judge shall have power to hold special Courts at his discretion. That the stated district Court shall be held at the places following, to wit: in the district of Maine, at Portland and Pownalsborough alternately, beginning at the first, in the district of New Hampshire, at Exeter and Portsmouth, alternately, beginning at the first, in the district of Massachusetts, at Boston and Salem alternately, beginning at the first, in the district of Connecticut alternately at Hartford and New Haven beginning at the first, in the district of New York at New York, in the district of New Jersey alternately at New Brunswick and Trenton beginning at the first, in the district of Pennsylvania at Philadelphia and York Town alternately beginning at the first, in the district of Delaware alternately at New Castle and Dover beginning at the first, in the district of Maryland alternately at Baltimore and Easton beginning at the first, in the district of Virginia alternately at Richmond and Williamsburgh beginning at the first, in the district of Kentucky at Harrodsburgh, in the district of South Carolina at Charleston, and in the district of Georgia alternately at Savannah and Augusta beginning at the first, — And that the special Courts shall be held at the same place in each district as the stated Courts, or in districts that have two or either of them at the discretion of the judge, or at such other place in the district, as the nature of the business and his discretion shall direct. And that in the districts that have but one place for holding the district Court, the records thereof shall be kept at that place, and in districts that have two, at that place in each district which the judge shall appoint.

*And be it further enacted,* That the before mentioned districts except those of Maine and Kentucky shall be divided into three circuits, and be called the eastern, the middle, and the southern circuit. That the eastern circuit shall consist of the districts of New Hampshire, Massachusetts, Connecticut, and New York, that the middle circuit shall consist of the districts of New Jersey, Pennsylvania, Delaware, Maryland and Virginia, and that the southern circuit shall consist of the districts of South Carolina and Georgia, and that there shall be held annually in each district of said circuits two Courts, which shall be called circuit Courts, and shall consist of any two Justices of the Supreme Court, and the district judge of such districts, any two of whom shall constitute a quorum: *Provided,* That no district judge shall give a vote in any case of appeal or error from his own decision, but may assign the reasons of such his decision.

*And be it further enacted,* That the first session of the said circuit Court in the several districts shall commence at the times following, to wit, in New Jersey on the second, in New York on the fourth, in Pennsylvania on the eleventh, in Connecticut on the twenty second, and in Delaware on the twenty seventh days of April next, in Massachusetts on the third, in Maryland on the seventh, in South Carolina on the twelfth, in New Hampshire on the twentieth, in Virginia on the twenty second, and in Georgia on the twenty eighth days of May next, and the subsequent sessions in the respective districts on the like days of every sixth calendar month afterwards, except in South Carolina where the session of the said Court shall commence on the first, and in Georgia where it shall commence on the seventeenth day of October, and except when any of those days shall happen on a Sunday, and then the session shall commence on the next day following. And the sessions of the said circuit Court shall be held in the district of New Hampshire at Portsmouth and twice in every year, beginning at the first, in the district of Massachusetts at Boston, in the district of Connecticut alternately at Hartford and New Haven beginning at the last, in the district of New York alternately at New York and Albany beginning at the first, in the district of New Jersey at Trenton, in the district of Pennsylvania alternately at Philadelphia and York Town beginning at the first, in the district of Delaware alternately at New Castle and Dover beginning at the first, in the district of Maryland alternately at Annapolis and Easton beginning at the first, in the district of Virginia alternately at Charlottesville and Williamsburgh beginning at the first, in the district of South Carolina alternately at Columbia and Charleston beginning at the first, and in the district of Georgia alternately at Savannah and Augusta beginning at the first. And the circuit courts shall have power to hold special sessions for the trial of criminal causes at any other time at their discretion, or at the discretion of the Supreme Court.

And be it further enacted, That the Supreme Court may, by any one or more of its Justices being present, be adjourned from day to day until a quorum be convened, and that a circuit court may also be adjourned from day to day by any one of its Judges, or if none are present by the Marshal of the district, until a quorum be convened, and that a district court, in case of the inability of the judge to attend at the commencement of a session, may by virtue of a written order from the said judge directed to the Marshal of the district, be adjourned by the said Marshal to such day, antecedent to the next stated session of the said court, as in the said order shall be appointed, and in case of the death of the said Judge, and his vacancy not being supplied, all process, pleadings, and proceedings of what nature soever, pending before the said court, shall be continued of course until the next stated session after the appointment and acceptance of the office by his successor.

And be it enacted, That the Supreme Court, and the district courts, shall have power to appoint Clerks for their respective courts, and that the Clerk for each district court shall be Clerk also of the circuit court in such district, and each of the said clerks shall, before he enters upon the execution of his office, take the following oath or affirmation, to wit, "I, A.B. being appointed Clerk of         do solemnly swear, or affirm, that I will truly and faithfully enter and record all the orders, decrees, judgments, and proceedings of the said court, and that I will faithfully and impartially discharge and perform all the duties of my said office, according to the best of my abilities and understanding. So help me God." Which words so help me God, shall be omitted in all cases where an affirmation is admitted instead of an oath. And the said Clerks shall also severally give bond with sufficient sureties (to be approved of by the Supreme and district courts respectively) to the United States in the sum of two thousand dollars, faithfully to discharge the duties of his office, and seasonably to record the decrees, judgments, and determinations of the Court, of which he is Clerk.

And be it further enacted, That the Justices of the Supreme Court, and the district judges, before they proceed to execute the duties of their respective offices, shall take the following oath or affirmation, to wit, "I, A.B. do solemnly swear or affirm, that I will administer justice without respect to persons, and do equal right to the poor and to the rich, and that I will faithfully and impartially discharge and perform all the duties incumbent on me as         according to the best of my abilities and understanding, agreeably to the constitution and laws of the United States. So help me God."

And be it further enacted, That the district courts shall have, exclusively of the courts of the several States, cognizance of all crimes and offences that shall be cognizable under the authority of the United States, committed within their respective districts, or upon the high seas, where no other punishment than whipping, not exceeding thirty stripes, a fine not exceeding one hundred dollars, or a term of imprisonment not exceeding six months, is to be inflicted. And shall also have exclusive original cognizance of all civil causes of admiralty and maritime jurisdiction, including all seizures under laws of impost, navigation or trade of the United States, where the seizures are made, on waters which are navigable from the sea by vessels of ten or more tons burthen, within their respective districts as well as upon the high seas. Saving to suitors, in all cases, the right of a common law remedy where the common law is competent to give it: And shall also have exclusive original cognizance of all seizures on land, or other waters, than as aforesaid made, and of all suits for penalties and forfeitures incurred, under the laws of the United States. And shall also have cognizance, concurrent with the courts of the several States, or the circuit courts, as the case may be, of all causes where an alien sues for a tort only in violation of the law of nations or a treaty of the United States. And shall also have cognizance, concurrent as last mentioned, of all suits at common law where the United States sue, and the matter in dispute amounts, exclusive of costs, to the sum or value of one hundred dollars. And shall also have jurisdiction exclusively of the Courts of the several States, of all suits against Consuls or Vice Consuls, except for offences above the description aforesaid. And the trial of issues in fact, in the district courts, in all causes except civil causes of admiralty and maritime jurisdiction, shall be by jury.

And be it further enacted, That the district court in Kentucky district shall, besides the jurisdiction aforesaid, have jurisdiction of all other causes, except of appeals and writs of error, herein after made cognizable in a circuit court, and shall proceed therein in the same manner as a circuit court. And writs of error and appeals shall lie from decisions therein to the Supreme Court in the same causes, as from a circuit court to the Supreme Court, and under the same regulations. And the district court in Maine district, shall besides the jurisdiction herein before granted, have jurisdiction of all causes, except of appeals and writs of error herein after made cognizable in a circuit court, and shall proceed therein in the same manner as a circuit court: And writs of error shall lie from decisions therein to the circuit court in the district of Massachusetts in the same manner as from other district courts to their respective circuit courts.

And be it further enacted, That the circuit courts shall have original cognizance, concurrent with the courts of the several States, of all suits of a civil nature at common law or in equity, where the matter in dispute exceeds, exclusive of costs, the sum or value of five hundred dollars, and the United States are Plaintiffs or Petitioners, or an alien is a party, or the suit is between a citizen of the State where the suit is brought, and a citizen of another State. And shall have exclusive cognizance of all crimes and offences cognizable under the authority of the United States, except where this Act otherwise provides, or the laws of the United States shall otherwise direct, and concurrent jurisdiction with the district Courts of the crimes and offences cognizable therein. But no person shall be arrested in one district for trial in another, in any a Justice of the Supreme or a Judge of a district Court, for an offence not punishable with death, shall afterwards procure bail, and there be no Judge of the United States in the district to take the same, it may be taken by any Judge of the Supreme, or Superior Court of Law of such State.

And be it further enacted, That the laws of the several States, except where the Constitution, treaties or statutes of the United States shall otherwise require or provide, shall be regarded as rules of decision in trials at common law in the Courts of the United States in cases where they apply.

And be it further enacted, That in all the Courts of the United States, the parties may plead and manage their own causes personally or by the assistance of such counsel or attorneys at law as by the rules of the said Courts respectively shall be permitted to manage and conduct causes therein. That there shall be appointed in each district a meet person, learned in the law, to act as Attorney for the United States in such district, who shall be sworn or affirmed to the faithful execution of his office, whose duty it shall be to prosecute in such district all delinquents for crimes and offences, cognizable under the authority of the United States, and all civil actions in which the United States shall be concerned, except before the Supreme Court in the district in which that Court shall be holden. And he shall receive as a compensation for his services such fees as shall be taxed therefor in the respective Courts before which the suits or prosecutions shall be. And there shall also be appointed a meet person, learned in the law, to act as Attorney General for the United States, who shall be sworn or affirmed, to a faithful execution of his office, whose duty it shall be to prosecute and conduct all suits in the Supreme Court in which the United States shall be concerned, and to give his advice and opinion upon questions of law when required by the President of the United States, or when requested by the heads of any of the departments, touching any matters that may concern their departments, and shall receive such compensation for his services as shall by law be provided.

Frederick Augustus Muhlenberg, Speaker of the House of Representatives.

John Adams, Vice President of the United States, and President of the Senate.

Approved September the Twenty fourth 1789

G. Washington, President of the United States

## For Further Reading:

Cooke, Jacob E., ed. *The Federalist*, nos. 78-83. Middletown, CT: Wesleyan University Press, 1961.

Goebel, Julius, Jr. *Antecedents and Beginnings to 1801*, chapter 11. Volume I of the *Oliver Wendall Holmes Devise History of the Supreme Court of the United States*. New York: Macmillan, 1971.